PHILIP GLASS
FIRST CLASSICS
1968-1969

Edition and introductory notes by Keith Potter

CHESTER MUSIC

DU10813

ISBN 9-78184-772-962-0
© 2010 Chester Music Ltd.

Cover designed by Fresh Lemon.

Cover image: Chuck Close b. 1940, *Phil,* 1969
Synthetic polymer on canvas, 108 x 84 in. (274.32 x 213.36 cm)
Whitney Museum of American Art, New York;
Purchased with funds from Mrs. Robert M. Benjamin 69.102
Photograph by Ellen Page Wilson, courtesy PaceWildenstein, New York
© Chuck Close, courtesy PaceWildenstein, New York

Music engraving by Jon Bunker
Published in Great Britain by Chester Music Limited
Head office:
14-15, Berners Street,
London W1T 3LJ
England

Sales and hire:
Music Sales Distribution Centre,
Newmarket Road,
Bury St. Edmunds,
Suffolk IP33 3YB,
England

www.chesternovello.com

All Rights Reserved.
Printed in Great Britain.

No part of this publication may be copied or reproduced
in any form or by any means without the prior permission
of Chester Music Limited.

CONTENTS

Introductory Note 4

Discography and Bibliography 7

1 + 1 8

Two Pages 10

Music in Fifths 15

Music in Contrary Motion 22

Music in Similar Motion 35

INTRODUCTORY NOTE

The five works included in this volume were composed by Philip Glass in New York between November 1968 and November 1969. For several years before that - first in Paris, where he had been studying with Nadia Boulanger, then on his travels in North Africa, Central Asia and, in particular, India, before his return to the USA in the summer of 1967 - the composer had been exploring "minimalist" means of writing music. Glass's minimalist approach was inspired partly by non-Western musical models but also by new discoveries he made around this time, including non-Western theatrical traditions and recent developments in experimental theatre. Among the former was the Kathakali theatre of south India; among the latter, the plays of Samuel Beckett and the productions of the Living Theater and Mabou Mines troupes, with the last of which the composer himself worked extensively.

Pre-eminent among Glass's non-Western musical influences were the traditions of both North Indian and, later, South Indian classical music, with their very different approaches to rhythm from that common in the West. Based on the accretion of small units to make larger ones, rather than on the Western method of taking "a length of time and [slicing] it the way you slice a loaf of bread", as Glass himself put it, Indian music works on the principle of addition, as opposed to Western music's basis in division.

Glass's development in the mid 1960s was further inspired by the example of some of the minimalist sculptors, painters and even film-makers, including Richard Serra and Michael Snow, whose work brought about the arrival of term minimalism in the first place. And this move was also encouraged by the example of other composers whose back-to-basics approach - likewise achieved via an intimate knowledge of various non-Western musics, especially that of India - has similarly been termed minimalist: notably La Monte Young, Terry Riley and Steve Reich.

The principle of additive rhythm revolutionised the way in which Glass thought about composition. Between 1965 and 1968, and particularly for about a year from the summer of 1967 onwards, following his return to the States that spring, he experimented – in works such as *Strung Out* for solo amplified violin (1967) and *Gradus* for soprano saxophone (1968) - with various kinds of additive and cyclic procedures which, however elaborately they built their musical structures on the gradual accretion of individual rhythmic units, remained essentially intuitive and non-systematic in their overall approach.

But it was only with the composition of *1 + 1* in November 1968 that Glass finally discovered the technique of what may be called "rigorous additive process": a more systematic deployment of minimalism allowing him to write music that proved a more successful adumbration of the minimalist aesthetic. For one thing, each work is now much more readily followable as a musical structure, and is arguably more likely to remain compelling from moment to moment. Since compositional process and sounding music become one, as it were, many of the aesthetic and practical aims of minimalism - including the concern to focus on sensations based on the direct perception of objects, encouraging a radical reconsideration of those objects - are much more completely achieved. For another, these scores are much more efficiently notated than the sometimes cumbersome ones that had immediately preceded them. As a consequence, they are also much more easily rehearsed and played, tricky though they still are to perform well. Though his minimalist scores predating *1 + 1* have their own attractions, and have recently begun to gain the attention of more performers, it is with the exploitation of rigorous schemes of additive and subtractive process in his compositions immediately following *1 + 1* that Glass arrives at a real maturity with his own individually minimalist means.

A few words each on the evolution of Glass's music during 1969; on the materials on which the scores now published here more formally for the first time are based; on instrumentation; and on performance spaces and amplification. Then, finally, lists of the available recordings of these compositions, which the would-be performer of them would be well advised to seek out, and a brief bibliography: not a comprehensive account of the now burgeoning scholarly literature on and around Glass's early minimalist scores, but simply a list of published sources mentioned in these notes and sufficient reference details for the curious reader to be able to find them.

Glass's Compositional Development During 1969

A gradual process of evolution will be observed in the five scores contained in this volume. The pitchless rhythmic minimalism and improvised structure of *1 + 1* gave Glass the main building blocks from which the monody of *Two Pages* (February 1969), his first mature minimalist composition, was constructed. The work's title is itself a celebration of the notational economy offered by a systematic application of additive process. According to Reich, who was working closely with the composer during this period, Glass originally headed the score *"Two Pages for Steve Reich"*; Glass himself simply reports that Reich liked *Two Pages* so much in rehearsal that he appended the words "for Steve Reich" to a score and presented it to him, never intending this as anything more than the spontaneous gift of a copy.

The bald consecutive perfect fifths of *Music in Fifths* (June 1969) are then followed by the two-part, limited counterpoint of *Music in Contrary Motion* (July 1969). Finally, the much more richly-textured *Music in Similar Motion* (November 1969) offers not only a quite complex range of different types of parallel motion but also, for the first time in the composer's mature scores, notes in the bass clef that betoken not only a warmer, more dense texture but also a hint of the harmonic progressions that were to invade Glass's scores by stealthy slow stages until they were revealed more openly in the operas *Einstein on the Beach* (1975) and *Satyagraha* (1980).

The composer's own account – given in the course of an interview with the present writer and Dave Smith in 1975 (see the short bibliography at the end of these introductory notes) - of how and why his music developed as it did at this time is refreshingly idiosyncratic and direct. It draws a connection between his own development in the late 1960s and Western art music's historical expansion from plainchant to *organum* and onwards to more elaborate contrapuntal forms:

My reasons for writing pieces were often very strange ... *Two Pages,* you remember, is in unison. Someone asked me if I was attempting to trace the progress of musical history and if, therefore, my next piece would follow on logically and be fifths. So I wrote *Music in Fifths.* That was all in parallel motion, so I obviously had to do one in contrary motion next. And after *Music in Contrary Motion* came its opposite again, *Music in Similar Motion.* It was a very easy going thing. In 1969 nobody knew me or cared much what I wrote, so I could make any jokes I liked.

Each of these compositions is constructed from a Basic Unit, which may vary in length from work to work and is usually easily divisible into two or more sub-units, which in turn may evolve independently. The scores themselves then simply notate the expansions and contractions of the Basic Unit that form the structure of each work, grouping these into figures of varying lengths without recourse to bar lines. Importantly, each of these figures is to be repeated an unspecified number of times before the next figure is reached.

Two Pages represents, as we have seen, Glass's first use of rigorous additive process in a composed-out score that is already quite sophisticated in the way it unwraps simple, audible processes. *Music in Fifths* adds not only a second line but also, initially, a less rigidly systematic structure; a degree of modal ambiguity but also metrical regularity enhance what is still ultimately, however, a perhaps less subtle score.

The additive and (more briefly) subtractive processes of *Music in Contrary Motion* are harder to follow than those of their two immediate predecessors, raising questions about the extent to which audibility of structure, an apparent "given" in early, hardcore minimalist music, is in practice pursued by the composer himself, and pursuable by the listener. Certainly, *Music in Similar Motion*, in some respects the most successful of these scores (and the only one to be retained in the Philip Glass Ensemble's repertoire after the early 1970s), piles up its lines to produce a more evolutionary rhythmic structure and a much more complex modality than can be found anywhere else in Glass's earliest minimalist compositions.

Materials

The source materials used in assembling this volume may be divided into three categories:

The composer's original manuscript scores: these, even when relying (as in all cases here) on photocopies of Glass's manuscript originals, can reasonably be taken as representing the composer's ideas about such scores at the time of their first performances. Since such copies were the versions from which each member of his own ensemble worked (there being no need of any separate parts for such simply notated scores), they have also sometimes had further performance indications added to them: mostly either structural clarifications to aid the performer, detailing the number of repetitions of each figure evidently decided on in rehearsal for a particular performance or performances, or details of the cueing used to move from figure to figure. (For more information on the repetitions of each figure, see the Performance Note for each work, particularly that for *Two Pages*, which outlines the general picture here as well.)

Previously published versions of scores based on the above manuscripts: despite the fact that Glass was for a long while reluctant to let any complete copies of his compositions into circulation, the first two of these five works have appeared at various times in other publications. More recently, all five have been available under separate cover on request from Dunvagen/Chester. Further brief details for each work are given individually under Sources, below.

Other scores: in addition to the above published scores, and "bootleg" copies of the composer's manuscript originals (which circulated in Britain from the early 1970s chiefly, it would seem, courtesy of the late Cornelius Cardew, who acted around this time, and earlier, as a catalyst for UK interest in American minimalism, amidst much else), particular mention should be made of the unpublished transcriptions of all five works here, except for the already fully available *1 + 1*, by the English composer and pianist, Dave Smith, made in 1974 and 1975, as their composer's own recordings of these works became available on LP. Enthusiastic to perform these compositions with his friend, John Lewis, and only partly satisfied by what he could obtain via Cardew (whom he knew well), Smith transcribed, and on a number of occasions, with Lewis, performed in public, *Two Pages*, *Music in Fifths* and *Music in Similar Motion*. The instrumentation for these performances was either two pianos or two electric keyboards. Smith also transcribed *Music in Contrary Motion*, but never played it outside rehearsals with Lewis. He also gave solo performances of *Two Pages*; and while Smith never played *Music in Fifths* as a solo, at least one other English composer-pianist, Andrew Poppy, did so.

The present edition of these works by Glass owes much to the assistance of Dave Smith: an old friend whose advice, based on intimate acquaintance with, and practical experience of, these scores, has been an important influence both on how they can best be presented in a user-friendly fashion to the player and on the performance notes that accompany them.

Instrumentation

The Philip Glass Ensemble emerged in the late 1960s out of a small group of players; most of the composer's early non-systematic minimalist scores were written for solo performers, as we have seen. By 1969, the group had expanded to, most often, three woodwinds (players doubling flutes and soprano saxophones) and three electric organs. Further expansion – the male voices of instrumental members of the ensemble, trumpet, several string instruments – came later, starting with *Music with Changing Parts* (1970); the only addition to survive beyond the early 1970s became the most important: a single female voice singing wordlessly.

All four works after *1 + 1* are written in an open-score format and, as we have already noted, they have also been performed by line-ups very different from that of Glass's own ensemble. All four appear to have been conceived at the keyboard, or are at least most easily played on keyboard instruments. Lying well under the hands and relying on considerable stamina, the evolving repeated patterns of some of these compositions can work well as solo keyboard performances, though the textural complexities of *Music in Similar Motion* cannot be achieved by anything less than a keyboard duo. For strings and, in particular, for all winds, the main problem is, as already suggested, sufficient energy and control to continue regular rhythmic patterns for long periods, and while the evidence of Glass's own recordings is that, even in such more controlled situations, he was forced to sanction individual players dropping out for short periods, it could be argued that this rarely works terribly well. The larger groupings, on the other hand, that would mask such disruptions are unlikely to maintain the clarity and ensemble control that these rhythmically and texturally very exposed scores require.

Small mixed groups, such as the composer's own sextet, as above, or solo, or duo interpretations, seem the answer. It would still, however, be interesting to try, say, a string-quartet version or even one for a small amplified vocal group. For more on how both precision and variety can be obtained within the confines of even a solo or duo performance, see the Performance Notes on each of these works below.

Performance Spaces and Amplification

Most of the early performances by the Philip Glass Ensemble took place in art galleries and other small spaces. Despite their size, but perhaps due in part to their acoustic idiosyncrasies, amplification was used from early on, though Kurt Munkacsi, responsible for refining the group's particular approach to amplified sound, did not join the ensemble until the autumn of 1970, after the works in this volume had been premiered.

But the main reasons for developing an amplified sound for the group were its deployment of electric keyboards, which necessitated electronic enhancement of any other instruments involved, and the desire to project the total ensemble sound at a high volume. Increasingly, and especially from *Music with Changing Parts* onwards, amplification was valued for enhancing the so-called psycho-acoustic effects that became an important feature of the experience of listening to this music: the illusions (of additional musical lines, including the effect of voices singing when there are no voices, to give just a single example) that can perhaps only be fully conjured up by fast repetition at a high dynamic level. Smith, though, suggests that the acoustics of the performing space, and accurate and consistent playing, are more important to revealing psycho-acoustic effects than sheer volume. It is certainly true that some features of these scores to which some would ascribe a psycho-acoustic dimension – such as the independent rhythms created by the iterations of single notes separated from the prevailing conjunct melodic motion by a perfect fourth or fifth (such as the low G in *Two Pages*) – can prove as notable in purely acoustic performances as in amplified ones. Performers are invited to explore this fascinating dimension of these scores for themselves.

Many performers attempting these scores will want to retain an amplified approach, which seems such a crucial part of the composer's sound world at this period. Other approaches are, however, up for exploration, as noted above. It should be observed, since "loud" is never added to the usual instruction of "fast, steady" in Glass's manuscript scores, that there is no reason why performances with a lower dynamic level should not be attempted; anything below *mp* is, though, likely to be tricky. The American group, Bang on a Can All-Stars, has done this to interesting effect with *Two Pages*. And while even amplified performances need not, of course, be loud, the most important, and unambiguous, requirement for the dynamic level of any performance of these works is that any volume initiated at the outset will be consistently and rigorously preserved throughout.

DISCOGRAPHY

Music in Fifths, Music in Similar Motion (Philip Glass Ensemble): Chatham Square 1003 (LP, 1973)
Two Pages [plus works by other composers] (Philip Glass and Michael Riesman): Folkways FTS 33902 (LP, 1975)
[Music in] Contrary Motion, Two Pages (same performance as the above) (Philip Glass and Michael Riesman): "Solo Music", Shandar 83 515 (LP, 1975)
Two Pages, Music in Fifths, [Music in] Contrary Motion and Music in Similar Motion (Philip Glass Ensemble): Elektra/Nonesuch 7559-79326-2 (CD, 1994), reissues of the above
1 + 1, Two Pages and [Music in] Contrary Motion [plus Mad Rush] (Steffen Schleiermacher): "Philip Glass: early keyboard music", Musikproduktion Dabringhaus und Grimm MDG 613 1027-2 (CD, 2001)
Music in Fifths, Music in Similar Motion [plus *How Now*) (Steffen Schleiermacher): "Philip Glass, How Now, Musikproduktion Dabringhaus und Grimm MDG 613 1600-2 (CD, 2010)

BIBLIOGRAPHY

Michael Nyman, *Experimental Music: Cage and beyond* (Cambridge: Cambridge University Press, 1999; original edition, 1974)
Dave Smith, "The Music of Phil Glass", *Contact*, no. 11 (Summer 1975), pp. 27-33
Keith Potter and Dave Smith, "Interview with Philip Glass", *Contact*, no. 13 (Spring 1976), pp. 25-30
Wes York, "Form and Process in *Two Pages* of Philip Glass", most easily found in Richard Kostelanetz, ed., *Writings on Glass: essays, interviews, criticism* (New York: Schirmer Books/London: Prentice Hall International, 1997/1999), pp. 60-79. York's article was first published in *Sonus*, vol. 1, no. 2 (Spring 1982), pp. 28-50
Philip Glass, ed., with supplementary material by Robert T. Jones, *The Music of Philip Glass* (New York: Harper and Row, 1987)/*Opera on the Beach* (London: Faber and Faber, 1988)
Keith Potter, *Four Musical Minimalists: La Monte Young, Terry Riley, Steve Reich, Philip Glass* (Cambridge: Cambridge University Press, 2000/2002)
Keith Potter, Geraint A. Wiggins and Marcus T. Pearce, "Towards Greater Objectivity in Music Theory: information-dynamic analysis of minimalist music", *Musicae Scientiae*, vol. 11, no. 2 (2007), pp. 295-324

1 + 1

(November 1968)

PERFORMANCE NOTE

The instructions given on this single-page score will be sufficient if it is borne in mind that it is more a blueprint or "kit" for assembling a performance than a score in any more conventional sense. Accordingly, the solo performer must first decide whether he or she wishes to prepare a written-out realisation in advance or improvise one at the moment of performance. Or, indeed, find some appropriate way of combining these two approaches: none of these alternatives appears prohibited by the composer's instructions.

Whatever solution is adopted, the player needs an understanding of the technique of additive (and subtractive) process in order to decide how any version will unfold. The essence of this process is simplest when, as in *1 + 1* and all the works that Glass composed in its immediate wake, it is also at its most severe and rigorous. While expansions and contractions of the two basic rhythmic units should probably be rigorously systematic, and not more loosely assembled, performers may like to explore the full range of interestingly different possibilities for elaborating these simple patterns.

Glass's score appears to insist on the application of fingers or knuckles to a table-top amplified by a contact microphone. In his book, *Experimental Music: Cage and beyond*, Michael Nyman suggests that other surfaces are also permitted, and it seems reasonable to advise that any combination of percussive agent, surface and mode of amplification that offers a similar result should be considered valid. Percussionists might like to investigate *1 + 1*; a performance on snare-drum, for example, might work well.

Steffen Schleiermacher, using a table-top in the only recorded performance so far available (released in 2001), offers two performances: the first at 5'25", the second at 2'30". The first of these expands and contracts the quaver unit around single iterations of two semiquavers and a quaver.

SOURCES

Dunvagen/Chester, but the complete single-page score was known for a long time via its appearances elsewhere, including in Nyman's already-mentioned *Experimental Music*; also later in the present editor's own *Four Musical Minimalists: La Monte Young, Terry Riley, Steve Reich, Philip Glass*. The original hand-written score, reproduced in both these publications, has been computer-set for the present volume.

1 + 1

for One Player and Amplified Table-Top

Any table-top is amplified by means of a contact mike, amplifier and speaker.
The player performs 1 + 1 by tapping the table-top with his fingers or knuckles.
The following two rhythmic units are the building blocks of 1 + 1:

1 + 1 is realized by combining the above two units in continuous, regular arithmetic progressions. Examples of some simple combinations are:

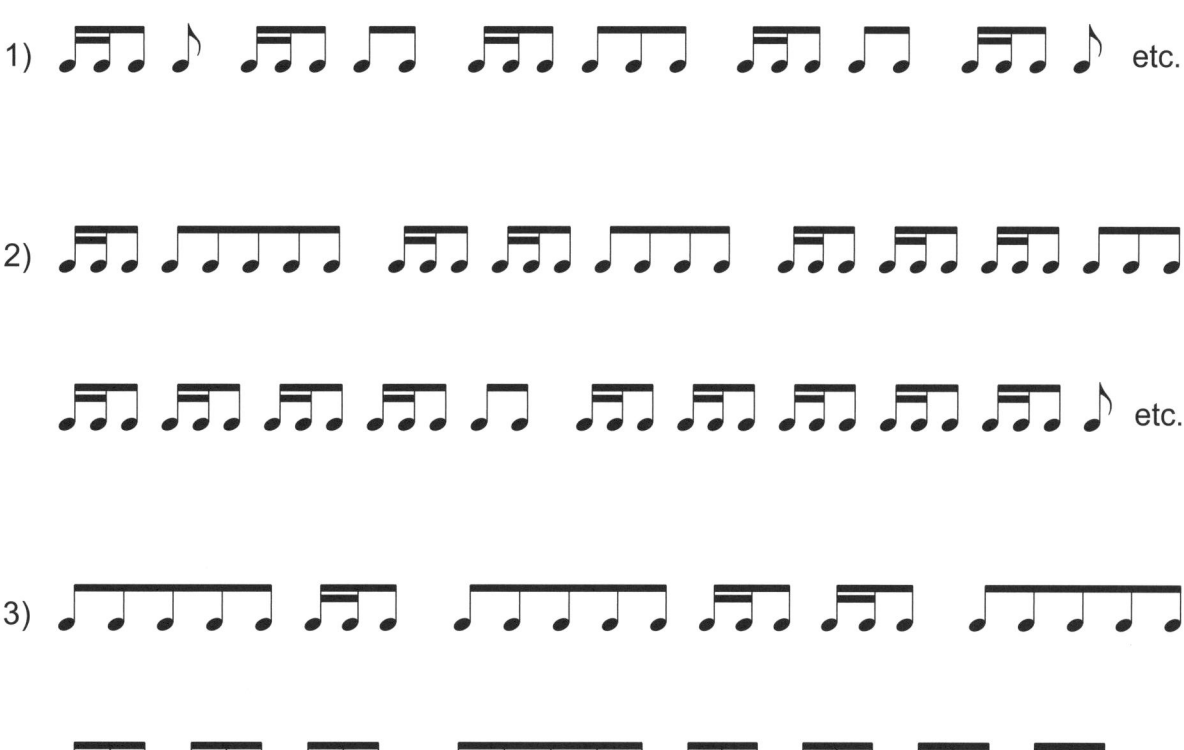

The tempo is fast. The length is determined by the player.

2

TWO PAGES

(February 1969)

PERFORMANCE NOTE

The basic instructions for Two Pages *also apply to the other three compositions that follow in this volume.*

Tempo: like the original scores of *Music in Fifths*, *Music in Contrary Motion* and *Music in Similar Motion*, the manuscript of *Two Pages* is simply marked "fast, steady". The composer's own original recording is at crotchet = c. 220. A marking of crotchet = 176 has been suggested for some of the works in this collection, but both the nature and the size of the instrumentation and the acoustics of the performance space are among the other factors that should also be taken into account when determining an appropriate speed that can be consistently maintained. For example, the clear attack of each note on a piano makes articulation and ensemble clarity easier at a faster speed than for many other instruments, so a performance for two pianos, or indeed a single piano, could operate at a higher tempo than one for a mixed ensemble. Smith's speeds for solo versions of *Two Pages* were a little faster than that of the Glass/Riesman recording.

Instrumentation and register: this is never specified on any of these four scores. Any combination of instruments whose range suits the material seems acceptable, and octave doubling, certainly at one octave below the notated pitch, would be a natural solution. A line-up similar to that used by the Philip Glass Ensemble – in the early days, when these works were written, usually three woodwinds (players doubling flutes and soprano saxophones) and three electric organs – appears appropriate. But Glass's 1975 recording of *Two Pages* is for a duo of electric organ and piano, and this work is especially suitable for a solo keyboard player, on piano, electric keyboard or even an organ of some kind. Schleiermacher's 2001 recording uses an electric organ.

The Glass/Riesman recording doubles an octave lower than the notated pitch (the impression of doubling an octave higher is probably psycho-acoustic). Doubling two octaves apart seems to Smith a good solution; in his solo version, he doubled two octaves below the notated pitch. With two keyboards, in the Smith/Lewis version, one piano, again, played at the notated pitch and two octaves lower, the other an octave above and below the notated pitch (as far as Smith can now recall).

Dynamics: instrumentation, arguably influenced by the fast tempo, has tended to ensure that most performances of *Two Pages* operate at a consistently high dynamic level. But see the Introductory Note, above, for possible alternatives.

Repetition of figures: each figure is to be repeated in an unbroken flow for a number of times to be determined by the players themselves. The number of repetitions of each figure may be fixed in advance, and the composer's manuscript indicates that his own ensemble at least sometimes, if not always, observed this practice. Glass's own solutions to this on the 1975 recording, as transcribed by Wes York, have been included in the version of *Two Pages* in this volume as an illustration of the composer's own practice. (See Sources, below.) These solutions are slightly different from those added to the manuscript score: unsurprisingly, since Glass doubtless explored various alternatives in different performances.

It should be emphasised that other performers of this score, as well as its companions here, should, in particular, regard these bracketed indications as merely an example of how these decisions might be made. As for the other works in this volume - for which no indications of repetition have been included in the scores themselves, only some further guidance in the Performance Note - players should come to their own decisions after also consulting, in addition, the guidelines in the next paragraph, below. Even the (unbracketed) details offered in this edition of the additive expansions and contractions from Figure 17 onwards (again, see also Sources, below) should be interpreted as one solution among several possible ones, not least since the composer's figure numbering of his original manuscript score cannot in all cases be made to tally with any application of additive process that is completely comprehensive and logical. The ambiguities inherent in the manuscript version for any performer not already well-versed in this performance practice have led to the decision to offer a more comprehensively written-out version for the present edition.

Two good general rules of thumb for deciding on the number of repetitions would be: the longer the figure, the fewer the repetitions; and the faster the overall tempo, the more repetitions. Whether fixed in advance or improvised, the move, also seamless, from one figure to the next is most easily achieved via an ensemble leader's nod of the head, indicating that the players should repeat the figure either once or twice more before proceeding. Glass's own practice seems mostly to have been "twice more". Smith, though, considers a single repetition following the nod to be clearer and less risky of misinterpretation; he concedes, though, that very short figures probably require "four more", since even two are insufficient. Interpreters are advised to experiment in rehearsal with what works best for them: the size and nature of the group, and its layout, will inevitably be factors to be taken into consideration here.

Overall length of performance: based on the composer's own practice in performance, a duration of between fifteen and twenty-five minutes is suggested for *Two Pages*. Glass's 1975 recording takes 17' 56", Schleiermacher's 2001 solo recording, however, takes 27' 25". Smith's solo performances timed at around seventeen minutes.

SOURCES

Dunvagen/Chester, in a version recopied by hand. But from 1982, Wes York's transcription of this work was available as part of an extended analysis of *Two Pages* that first appeared that year. Having been unable to obtain a score, York made his own transcription from the composer's 1975 recording. He included precise indications of the number of repetitions of each figure that Glass and his co-performer, Michael Riesman, had used in this performance: the present edition of *Two Pages* draws, as already indicated, on this valuable task in order to give a detailed example to intending performers, as well as intending scholars, of this music, of what sorts of decisions the composer himself has made on this subject. York's rich and complex analysis, which reveals just how subtle and complex this apparently simple work is, subsequently reappeared in two book-length collections of articles, first in 1985 and then in 1997; for details, see the brief bibliography on page 7.

The copy of the original manuscript score of *Two Pages,* the basis for the present computer-set version, uses an abbreviated notation for the additive expansions and contractions found from Figure 17 onwards. The more comprehensively written-out version for the present edition again draws on York's account, though performers wishing to experiment with the unfolding of the expansions and contractions might like to note that the 1975 recording offers an alternative example in Figures 17-39: instead of York's logical solution (offered in the present score) of increasing consecutively up to 10, then in twos up to 18, and back the same way, Glass and Riesman actually seem to have jumped from 12 to 18, then 20, before filling in 16 and 14 on the return. Any regrets that the version published here no longer fits neatly onto two pages seem overcome by confidence that the score should be user-friendly to anyone seriously contemplating a performance.

The source photocopy for this edition has also been annotated, almost certainly in the composer's own hand, in several ways, most notably with the numbers of repetitions of each figure apparently used for at least one performance. These are similar, though not identical, to those found on the Glass/Riesman recording and York's transcription of this.

Thanks are due to Wes York for permitting the reproduction of some details from his transcription of Two Pages.

TWO PAGES

3
MUSIC IN FIFTHS

(June 1969)

PERFORMANCE NOTE

Tempo: again, "fast, steady". The composer's own recording is at crotchet = c. 200. This seems likely to work well in some circumstances; but, as before, instrumentation and performance space should both play a role in determining the best speed. Smith and Lewis's speeds for duo versions of *Music in Fifths* were a little faster.

Instrumentation and register: again, any suitable combination of instruments. *Music in Fifths* was originally performed by the above ensemble of three woodwinds (players doubling flutes and saxophones) and three electric organs. Glass's 1973 recording is for a trio of two soprano saxophones and electric organ. Schleiermacher's 2010 recording uses a multi-tracked electric organ.

The "five-finger exercise" aspect of *Music in Fifths* (as Nyman once called it) may seem emphasised best by solo performances confined to the register as notated. Smith points out that the disorientation caused both by the purely scalic nature of the figures themselves and by their increasing length would render even duo performances tricky; the composer and his own expert musicians on the 1973 recording evidently found an ensemble performance difficult.

The Philip Glass Ensemble doubles the notated pitches an octave below on the 1973 recording. With just two keyboards, Smith and Lewis again used octave doubling. In their early performances, one piano played at the notated pitch and one octave lower. In their later performances, a solution considered better was devised: Piano 1 played the upper line at pitch and the lower line an octave below the notated pitch; Piano 2 played the upper line an octave lower and the lower line two octaves below the notated pitch. Smith says that he never did a solo performance, but if he had, he would have used the solution for Piano 2, above, opting for a lower-pitched version than actually notated.

Dynamics: as with *Two Pages*, a high dynamic level is common but not essential. The "experimental flatness" of these compositions, however, requires consistency of dynamics, as of everything else. And, inevitably, a loud performance will conform better to the description of *Music in Fifths* – made by Steve Reich, who played some of these works when they were new – as "like a freight train".

Repetition of figures: as for *Two Pages*. However, both the Philip Glass Ensemble and Smith/Lewis not only reduced the number of repetitions of the long figures in the work's later stages to just three or even two, but also restricted the repetitions of Figures 1-12: in Glass's own case, basically twice each, throughout what could be regarded as this introductory section; then a much larger number of repetitions of the short Figure 13. In Figures 4-12, it should be noted, the notation of the repeated "tag" within the internal structure of these figures has been amended by using simple repeat signs.

Overall length of performance: based on the composer's own practice in performance, a duration of between seventeen and twenty-five minutes is suggested for *Music in Fifths*. Glass's 1973 recording takes 23' 19", Schleiermacher's 2010 recording takes 22' 07". Smith and Lewis's duo performances timed at around twenty minutes.

SOURCES

Music in Fifths: Dunvagen/Chester only, in the composer's original hand-written score; extracts also reproduced in, e.g., Nyman 1974 and Potter 2000 (see bibliography). The original manuscript score occupies ten pages and much of its layout, with even spacing of notes and plenty of space between the lines, is preserved in the version included here.

MUSIC IN FIFTHS

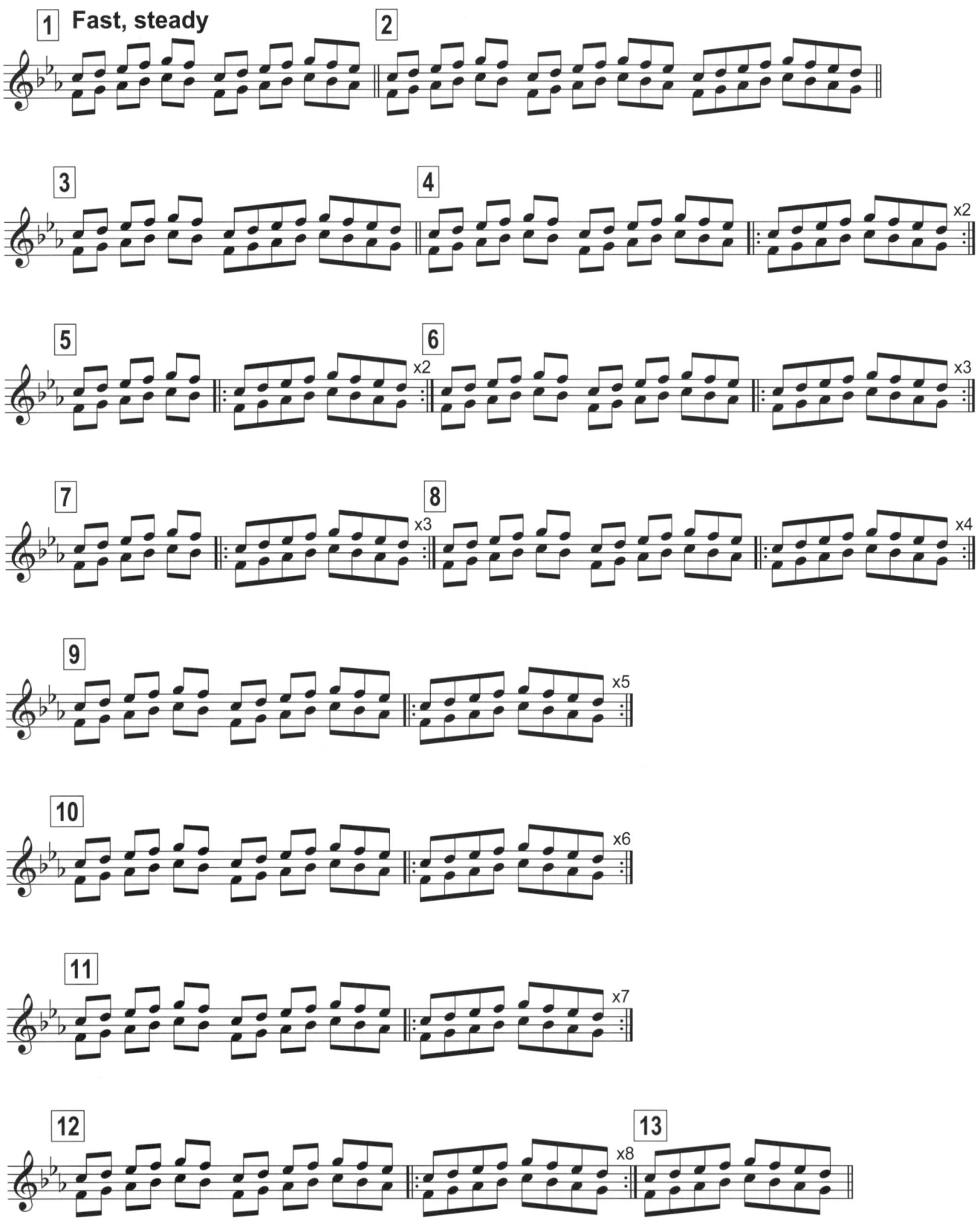

MUSIC IN CONTRARY MOTION

(July 1969)

PERFORMANCE NOTE

Tempo: once again, "fast, steady", with the advice given for *Music in Fifths*. The composer's own recording is at crotchet = c. 200.

Instrumentation and register: once again, any suitable combination of instruments. *Music in Contrary Motion* proved tricky as an ensemble work, and Glass's 1975 recording is a solo version for electric organ played by the composer himself. This crucially adds a pair of pedal points – one on A, the other on E (i.e. tonic and dominant) - though these are not indicated in the score. A underpins the first half of each figure, E the second half (but note the additional information under Sources, below). Schleiermacher's 2001 recording uses an electric organ.

Dynamics: as for the above works.

Repetition of figures: as for the above works; the length of the figures from 7, and especially 19, onwards suggests few repetitions, or even no repetitions at all.

Overall length of performance: based on the composer's own practice in performance, a duration of between twelve and twenty minutes is suggested for *Music in Contrary Motion*. Glass's own 1975 recording takes 15' 31". Schleiermacher is, as for *Two Pages,* longer, at 22' 12".

SOURCES

Music in Contrary Motion: Dunvagen/Chester only, in the composer's original hand-written score; extracts also reproduced in, e.g., Potter 2000 (see bibliography). The original manuscript score occupies fourteen pages and some of its layout, with even spacing of notes and plenty of space between the lines, is preserved in the version included here.

It should be stated here that Glass's 1975 recording differs from this previously published score in a curious way. The notation begins the Basic Unit in a different place in its unfolding to that chosen for the recording: if, for Figure 1, the score can be represented as $a + b + c + d + e + f$, with a scale-based pattern first, then the recording can be described as $c + d + e + f + a + b$. While the notated score, in the composer's own hand, might seem to have priority, it is, again, Glass himself who provides the alternative version, and evidence suggests that he played this version in concerts for several years. What appear to be the composer's own second thoughts, as conveyed via this recording, might be preferred musically.

MUSIC IN CONTRARY MOTION

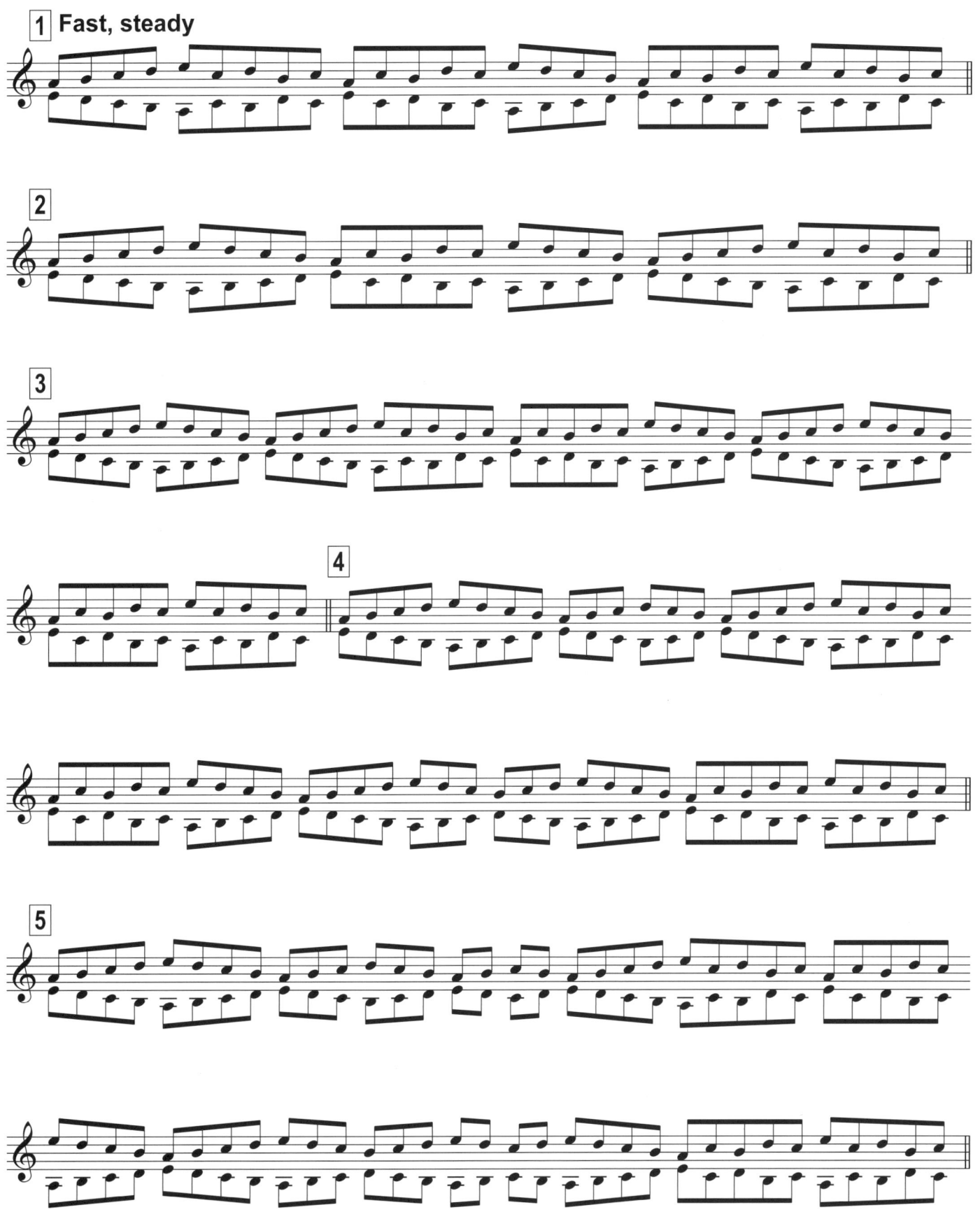

23

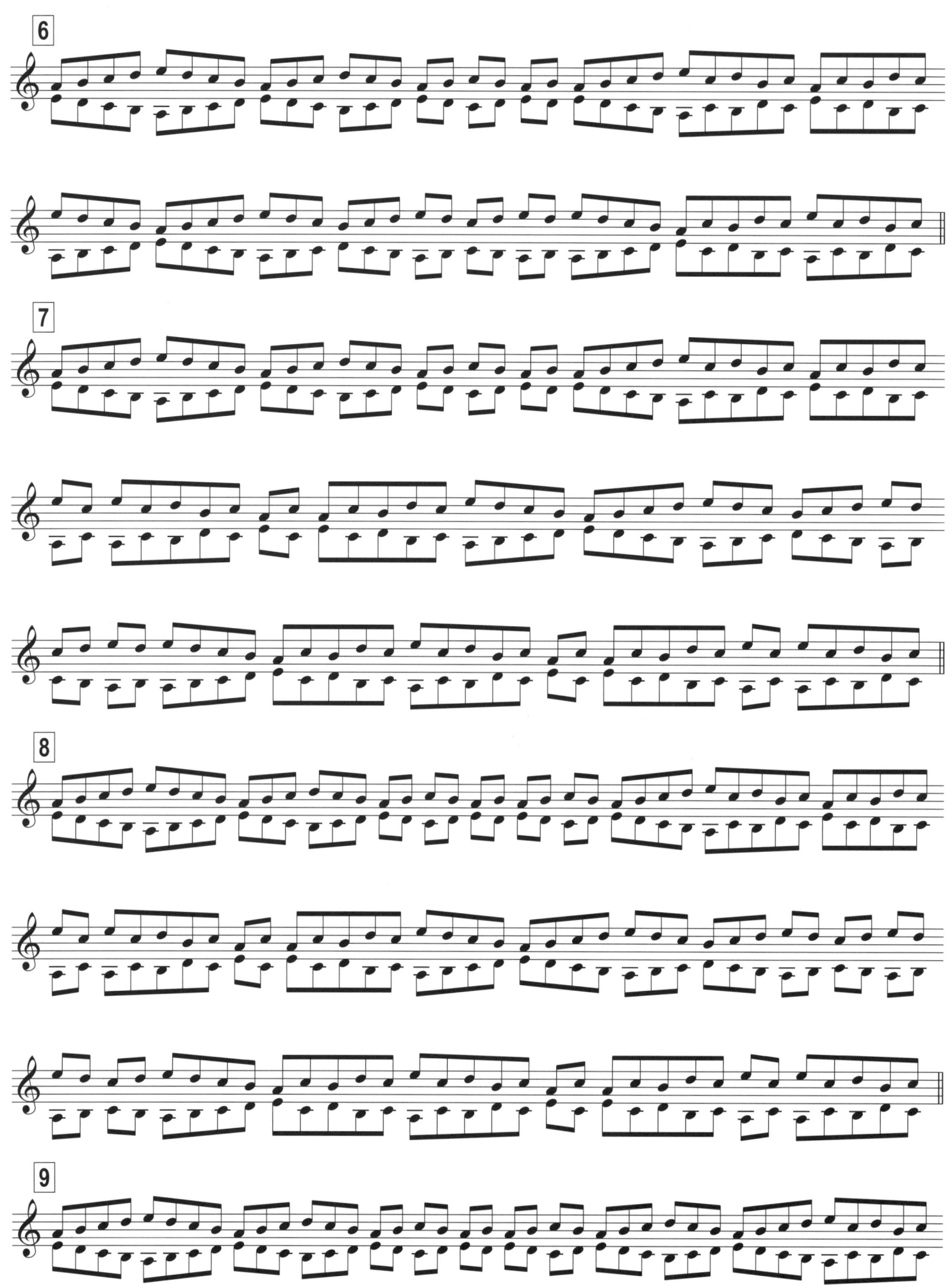

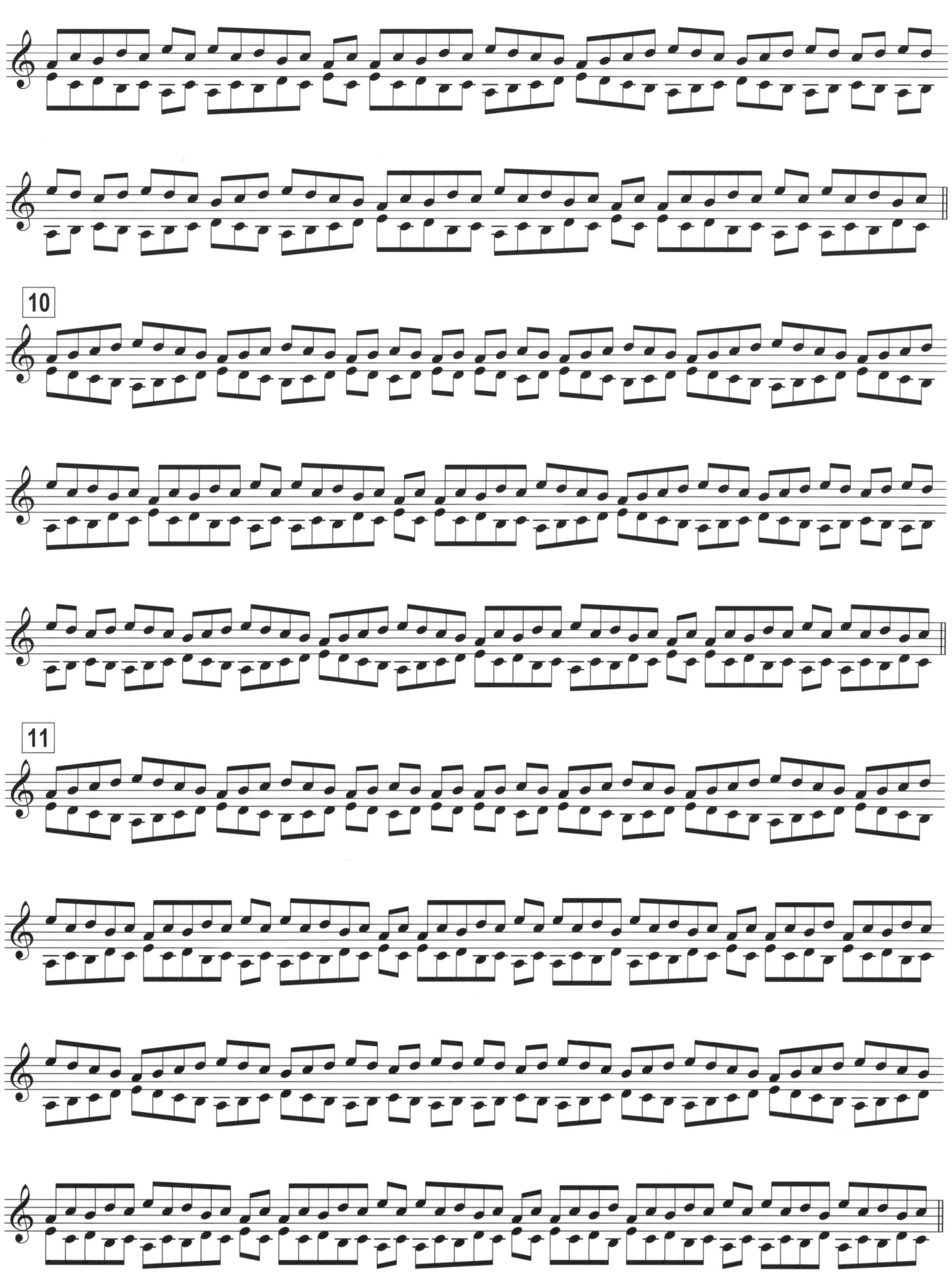

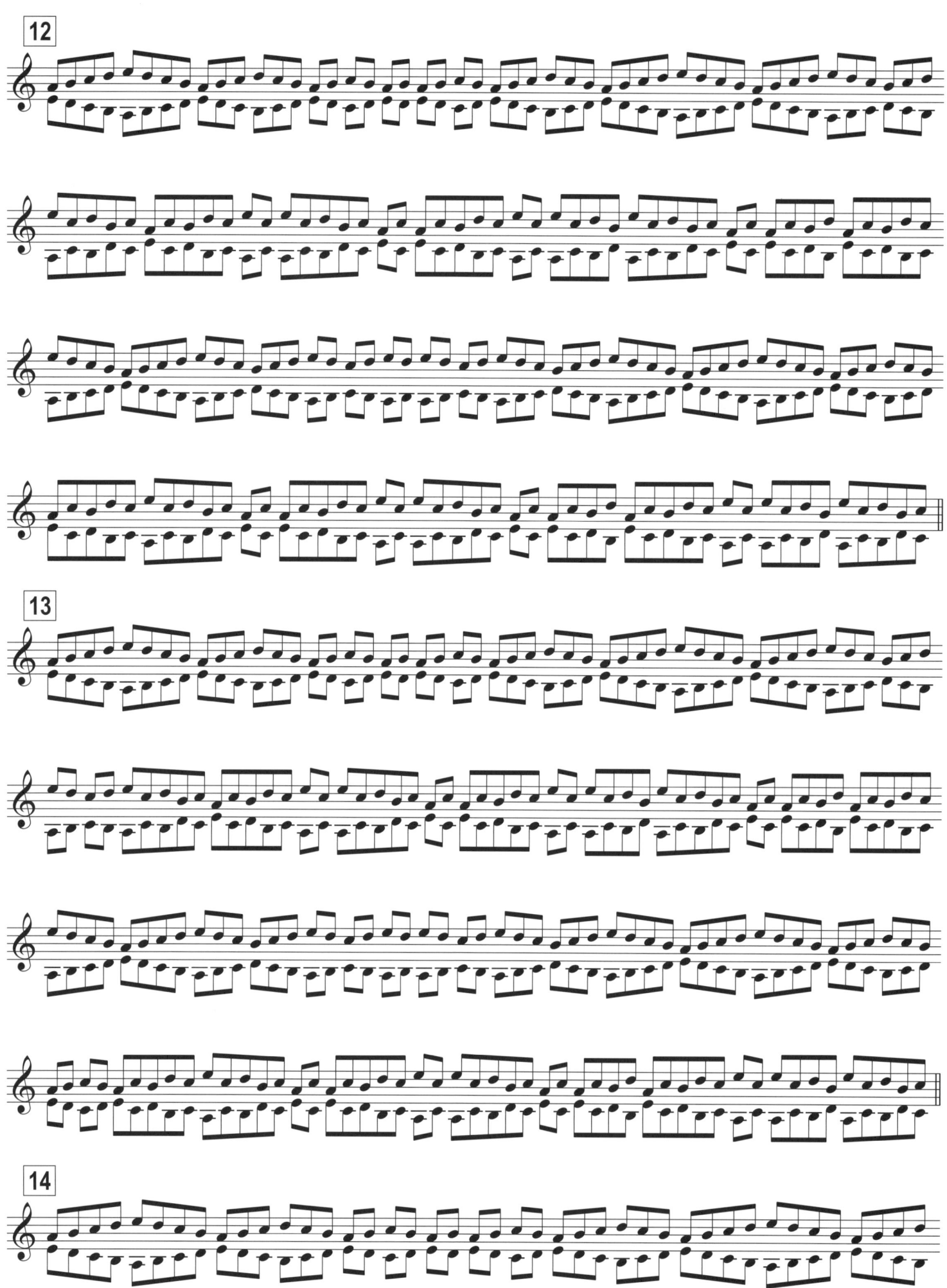

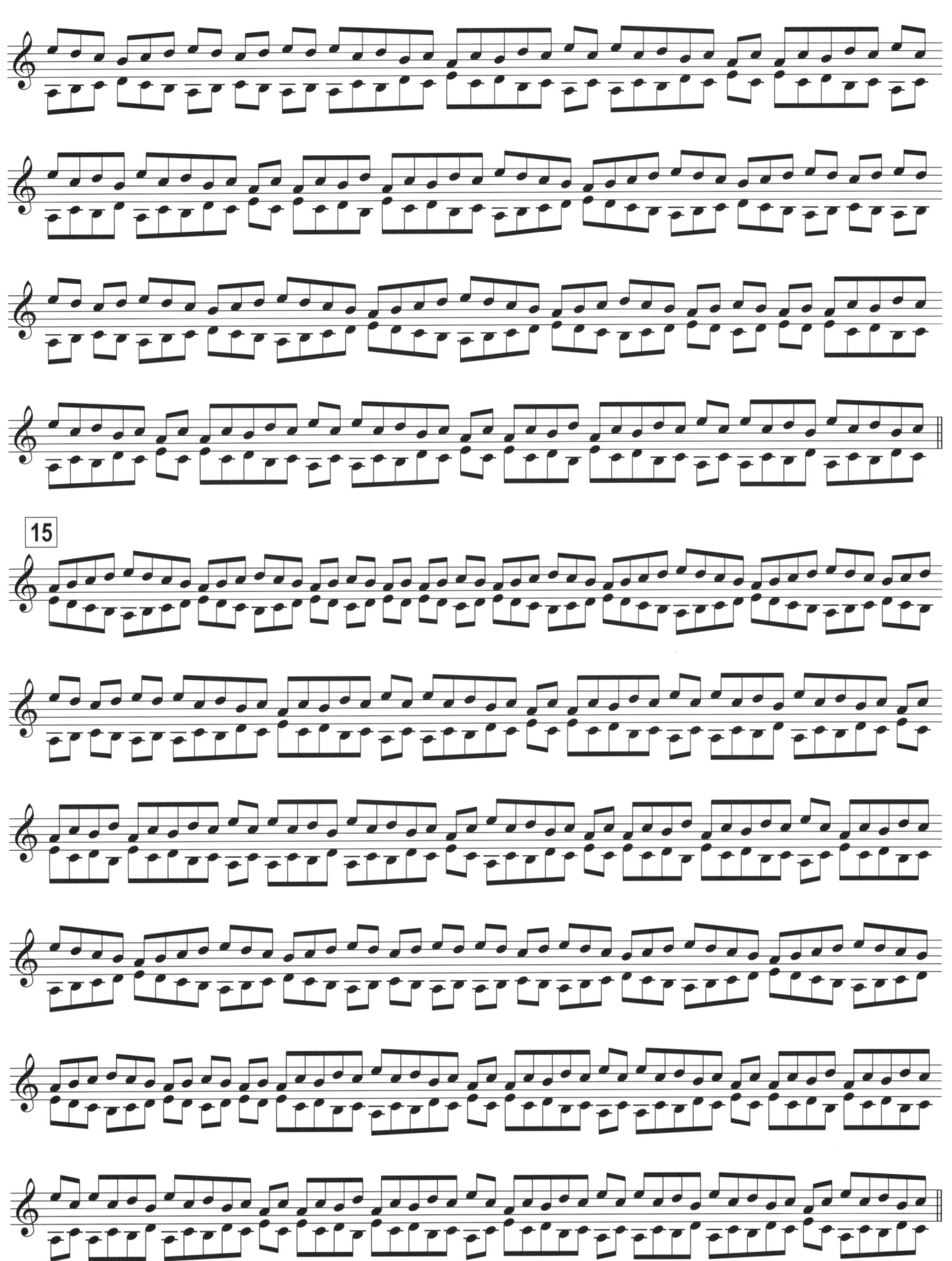

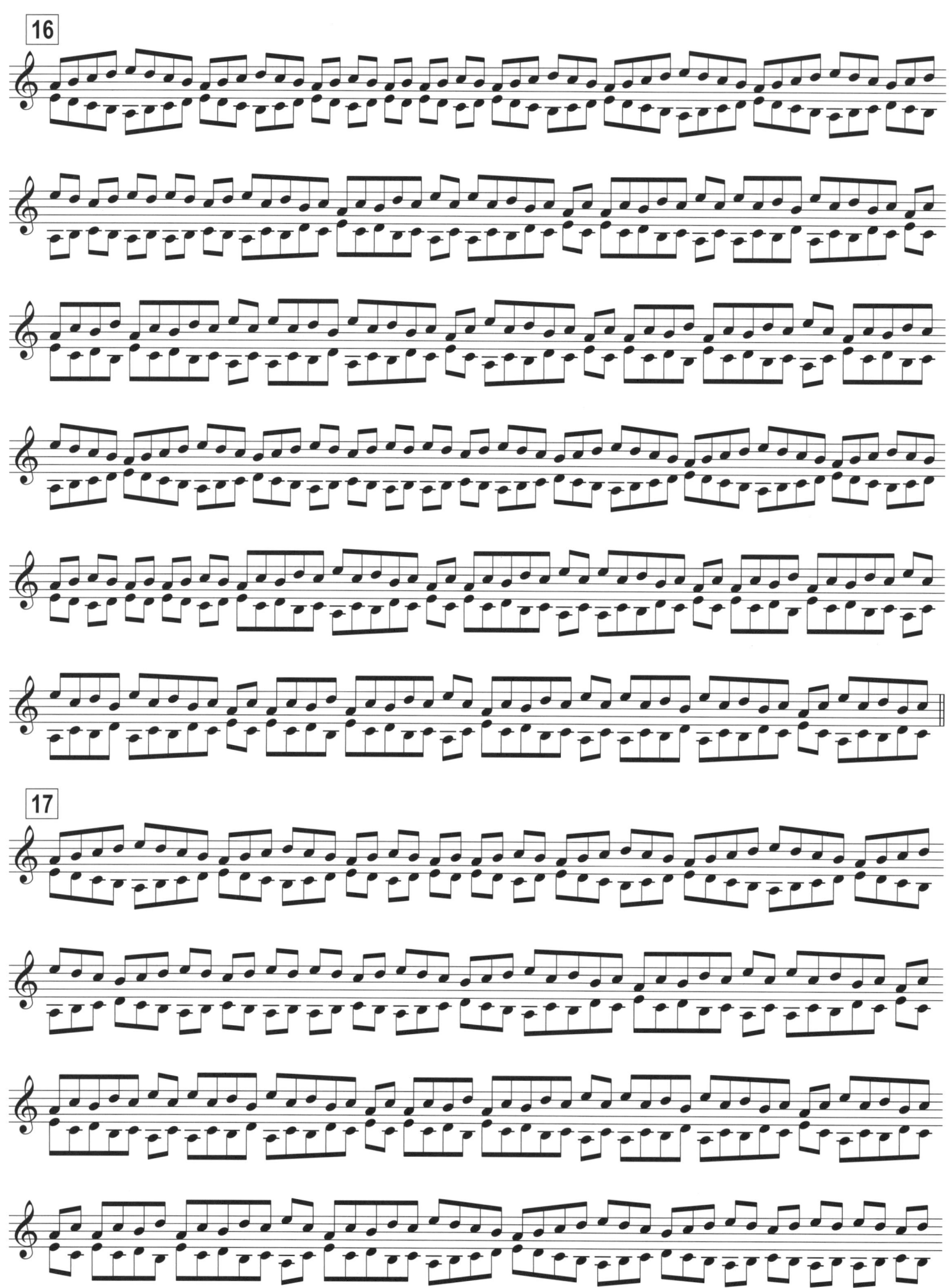

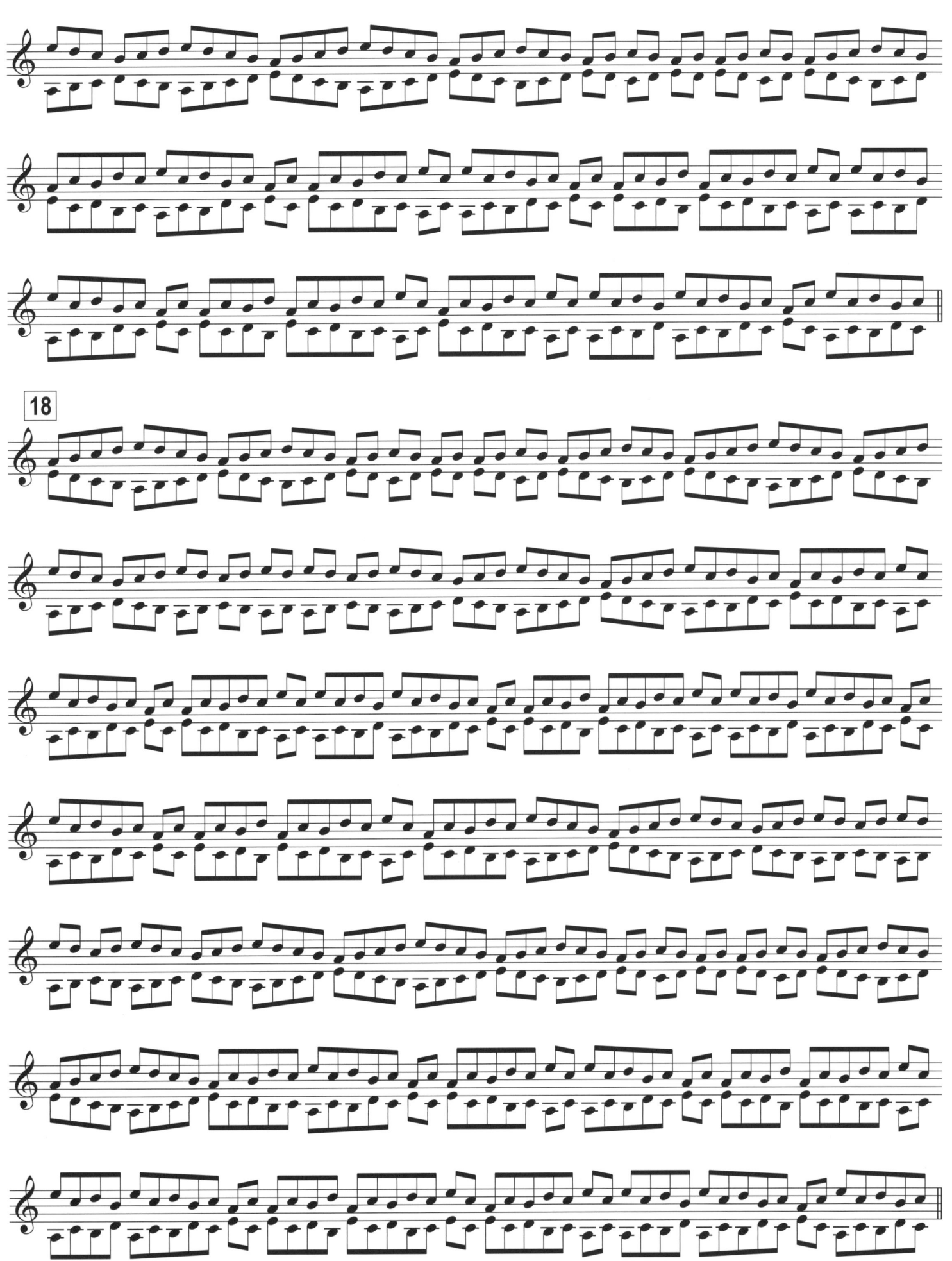

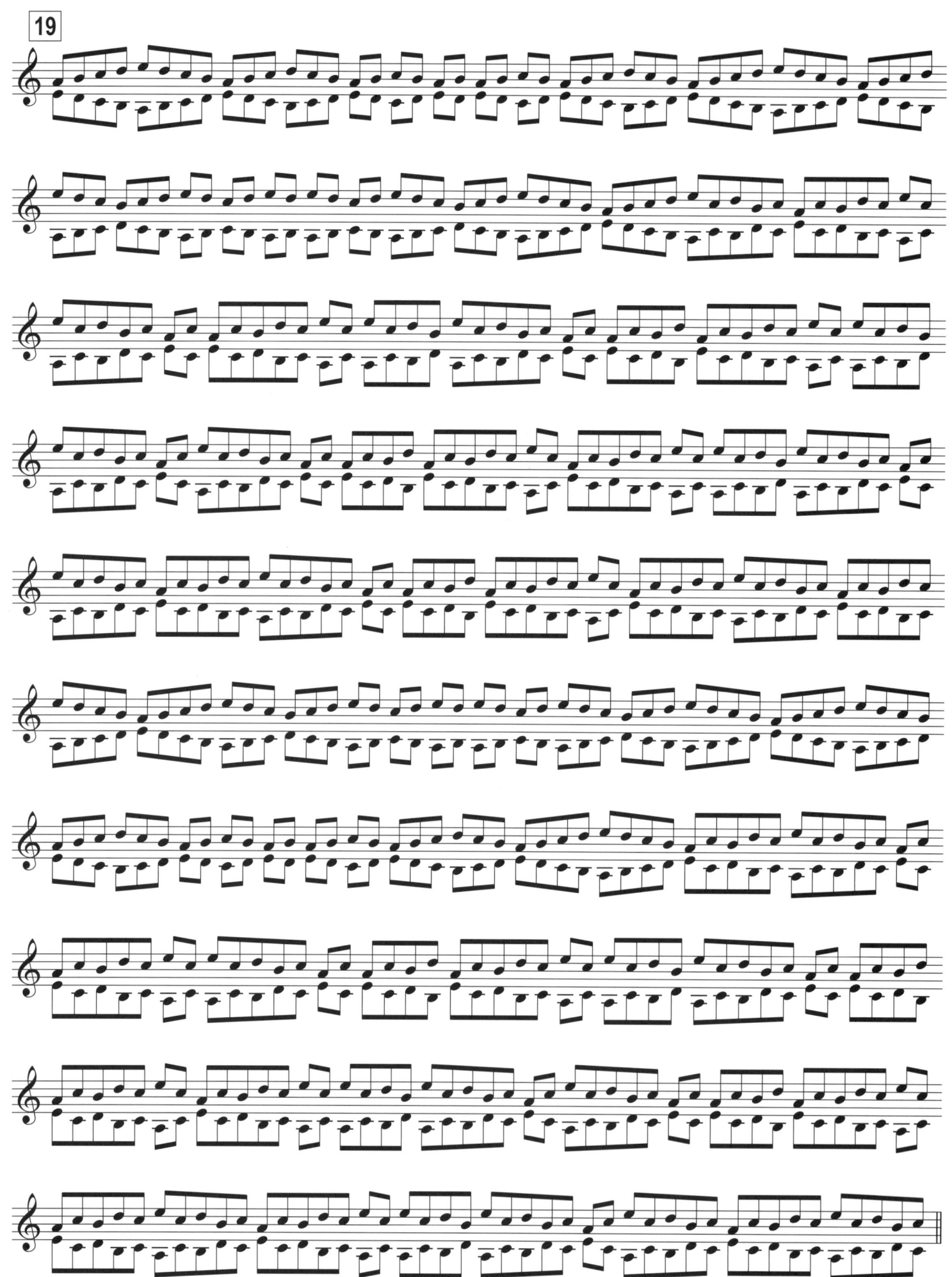

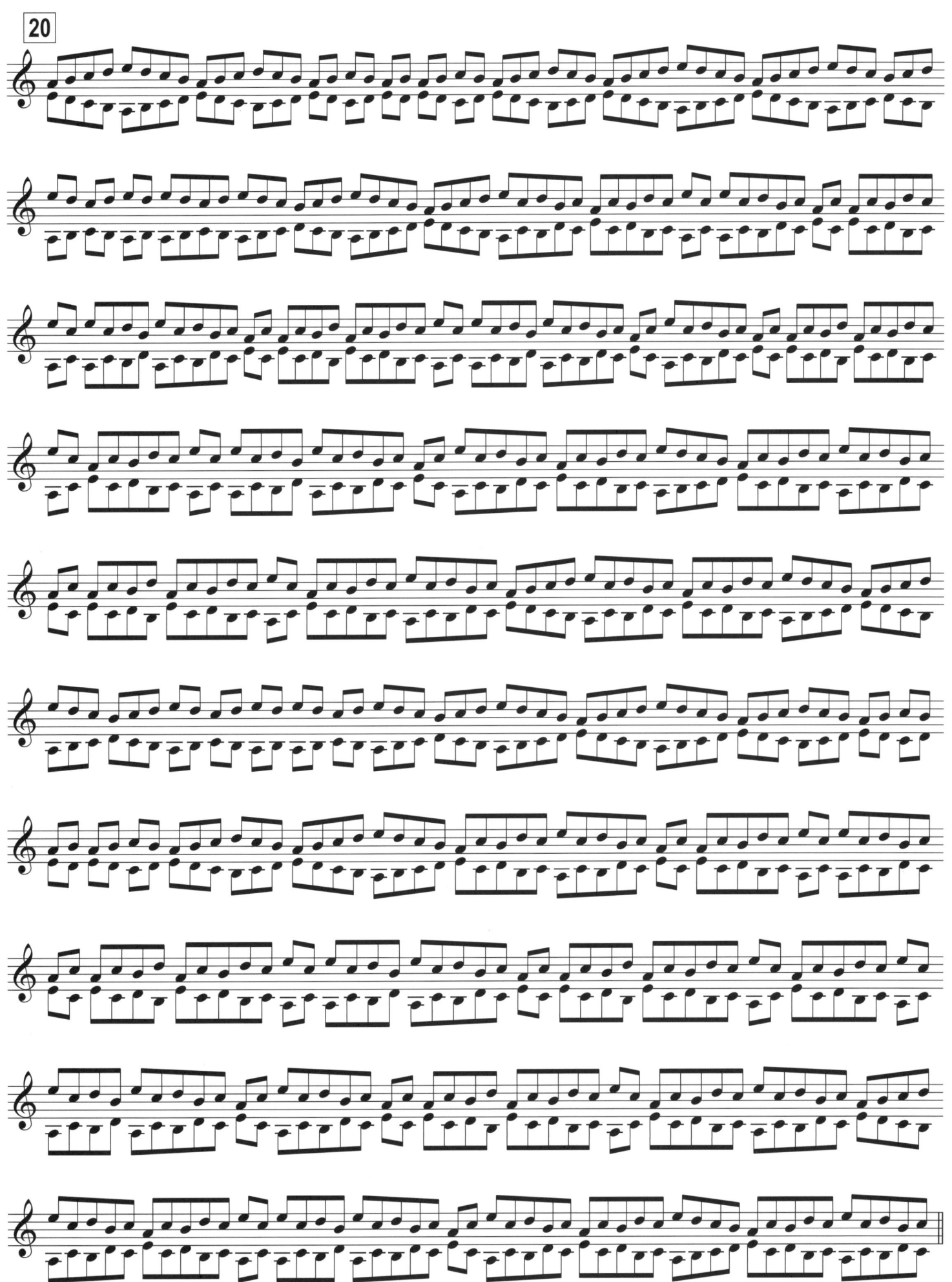

21

22

5

MUSIC IN SIMILAR MOTION

(November 1969)

PERFORMANCE NOTE

Tempo: again, "fast, steady", with the advice given for *Music in Fifths*. The composer's own recording is at crotchet = c. 190. The orchestral version gives a metronome marking of crotchet = ca. 120, perhaps sensible with much bigger forces. Smith and Lewis's speeds for duo versions of *Music in Similar Motion* were, as for *Music in Fifths*, a little faster than that of the Philip Glass Ensemble recording.

Instrumentation and register: again, any suitable combination of instruments. Glass's 1973 recording is for a fairly typical sextet of three woodwinds (this time, however, one flute and two soprano saxophones) and three electric organs. The addition of an explicit bass register for the first time in these scores suggests a fairly rich-textured ensemble. *Music in Similar Motion* cannot be performed as a straightforward solo; Schleiermacher's 2010 recording uses a multi-tracked electric organ. Smith's ingeniously-voiced arrangement for two pianos shows that this combination can work especially well. It depends, however, on dividing the upper line beginning on C between the two instruments, following the arrival of the final new upper line beginning on F (from Figure 24 onwards). The arrangement of Figure 24 in the example below demonstrates how this can be achieved; the Appendix following the main score itself offers a full elaboration of this from Figure 24 to the end.

Dynamics: as for the above works.

Repetition of figures: as for the above works.

Overall length of performance: based on the composer's own practice in performance, a duration of between fifteen and twenty minutes is suggested for *Music in Similar Motion*. Glass's 1973 recording takes 17' 11", Schleiermacher's 2010 recording takes 18' 14". The published orchestral version of the score suggests "from 15 to 18 minutes". Smith and Lewis's duo performances timed at around twenty minutes.

SOURCES

Music in Similar Motion: not previously available from Dunvagen/Chester; extracts reproduced in, e.g., Potter 2000 (see bibliography), which used Smith's arrangement for two pianos (see Instrumentation and register, above).

The original manuscript score, occupying four pages, is written on two staves, treble and bass. The initial single line, doubled at the octave, is joined from Figure 6 by another, doubling the initial line a perfect fourth above (starting on C), except for one pitch (G, rather than F) in the "cadential" figure that has by now been added to the opening figure. The upper octave of the initial line is omitted in the manuscript from here on as notationally superfluous, though it is clear both from the manuscript itself and from the composer's own recording that it also continues throughout. From Figure 12, an added bass line moves in similar, but not identically doubled, motion to the others, spanning a full octave, G-G, plus a low F for the "cadential" figure. Finally, from Figure 24 (an accidental mis-numbering in Glass's original manuscript score has been corrected in the present version), a further doubling in similar but not identical motion is introduced, supplying a fourth "real part" starting on F, a perfect fourth above C, in the treble stave. The parallel but not identically doubled lines of *Music in Similar Motion* give the work its name.

On Glass's 1973 recording, the number of repetitions of the four-note "cadential" figure is further expanded from 16 to 32 via the inclusion of an additional figure between the notated Figures 28 and 29. Though this occurs in neither of the composer's notated versions, including the orchestral arrangement discussed below, performers of *Music in Similar Motion* might enjoy exploring whether this extra expansion suits their own interpretation, as Glass clearly must have felt it did his in 1973. Schleiermacher's 2010 recording follows the composer's lead here, though I think that he falls slightly short of the full thirty-two repetitions of the "cadential" figure in Figure 28 before moving on to Figure 29.

Orchestral Arrangement by the Composer

A published version for orchestra was made by Glass himself in 1981 for performance by the American Composers Orchestra under Dennis Russell Davies (the editor of this volume heard the world premiere of the version in Paris in May that year); this has been available from Dunvagen/Chester since that time. The scoring is triple woodwind (but four clarinets and just two bassoons), four horns, two trumpets, two trombones and tuba, electric organ (or piano) and strings (strength unspecified).

This arrangement's basic strategy is the expected and inevitable one of accumulation by registral expansion, but some instruments are reassigned to new lines as these arrive, offering some variety to the individual orchestral parts. Thus the initial texture, formed by pairs of woodwind, plus cor anglais, organ and upper strings, of Figures 1-5 is retained with the arrival of the new line in similar motion at Figure 6, two flutes, but just a single oboe and clarinet, plus first violins, supplying the extra real part. Bass clarinet and cellos are added from Figure 12; then the full orchestra - including piccolo. E-flat clarinet and chordal reinforcement of the cadential figure from the brass section and double basses - with the arrival of the top line at Figure 24. A marking of *forte* is unambiguously given at the beginning of the score and again at Figure 24.

Such departures from the original score as the splendidly held notes of the four French horns in this arrangement's closing stages may not be appropriate to any but large-scale versions of *Music in Similar Motion*, and this orchestral arrangement is likely to prove too heavy and problematic to co-ordinate, especially on limited rehearsal time with players less than conversant with or sympathetic to Glass's style. It might, nevertheless, give intending performers of the work some ideas for deploying ensembles bigger than the composer's original sextet.

MUSIC IN SIMILAR MOTION

Appendix: possible arrangement for two-piano version of *Music in Similar Motion*.